T0151721

IMPROVISATION WITHOUT ACCOMPANIMENT

Winner, 2018 A. Poulin, Jr. Poetry Prize

Selected by Patricia Smith

IMPROVISATION
WITHOUT
ACCOMPANIMENT

POEMS BY

MATT MORTON

FOREWORD BY PATRICIA SMITH

A. POULIN, JR. NEW POETS OF AMERICA SERIES, NO. 44

BOA EDITIONS, LTD. ❧ ROCHESTER, NY ❧ 2020

First Edition
20 21 22 23 7 6 5 4 3 2 1

Publications by BOA Editions, Ltd.—a not-for-profit corporation under section 501 (c) (3) of the United States Internal Revenue Code—are made possible with funds from a variety of sources, including public funds from the Literature Program of the National Endowment for the Arts; the New York State Council on the Arts, a state agency; and the County of Monroe, NY. Private funding sources include the Max and Marian Farash Charitable Foundation; the Mary S. Mulligan Charitable Trust; the Rochester Area Community Foundation; the Ames-Amzalak Memorial Trust in memory of Henry Ames, Semon Amzalak, and Dan Amzalak; the LGBT Fund of Greater Rochester; and contributions from many individuals nationwide. See Colophon on page 84 for special individual acknowledgments.

Cover Design: Sandy Knight
Interior Design and Composition: Richard Foerster
BOA Logo: Mirko

Library of Congress Cataloging-in-Publication Data

Names: Morton, Matt, 1987- author. | Smith, Patricia, 1955- writer of foreword.
Title: Improvisation without accompaniment / poems by Matt Morton ;
  foreword by Patricia Smith.
Description: First edition. | Rochester, NY : BOA Editions, LTD., 2020. |
  Series: A. Poulin, Jr. new poets of America series; no. 44 | Summary: "Set in the
  backdrop of rural Texas, Matt Morton's debut poetry collection reaches for existential
  meaning within life's joys and griefs"— Provided by publisher.
Identifiers: LCCN 2019035667 (print) | LCCN 2019035668 (ebook) | ISBN
  9781942683957 (paperback) | ISBN 9781942683964 (ebook)
Subjects: LCGFT: Poetry.
Classification: LCC PS3613.O77867 I47 2020 (print) | LCC PS3613.O77867
  (ebook) | DDC 811/.6—dc23
LC record available at https://lccn.loc.gov/2019035667
LC ebook record available at https://lccn.loc.gov/2019035668

BOA Editions, Ltd.
250 North Goodman Street, Suite 306
Rochester, NY 14607
www.boaeditions.org
A. Poulin, Jr., Founder (1938–1996)

for Michael Adams

Contents

Foreword

Judging the Poulin (doesn't the simple "Poulin" elegantly resound like "Oscar," "Emmy," or "Tony"?) is an onerous undertaking. Anyone who says that poetry is sucking in its final dramatic breath—*again*—should, at least once, be confronted by a teetering stack of printouts, each manuscript purporting to be the urgent bellow of the utterly necessary.

And more than a few are just that.

Then there's "judging," which hints at some immediate, Zeus-like, overarching skill set bound to make a winner glaringly apparent. However, that's galaxies away from the actual process. While it's true that cream moseys to the top, there sometimes is lots and lots of cream and the top gets crowded. What's a judge to do?

In consideration on every page and in varying degrees: Technical mastery, unpredictable entry points, inventive form, control, a measured lack of control, history, pathos, influence, daring, sparkling syntax, surprise, tugging of heartstrings, laughter (both the suppressed giggle and head-thrown-back versions), wonder, familiarity, and—I believe the technical term is *hook me, dammit, with lines that won't leave.*

In the gorgeous and deftly-wrought "Elegy for My Brother in the Wilderness"—a sectioned masterwork that, in my eyes, anchors this remarkable winning collection—Matt Morton writes, "The manner in which one begins is of utmost importance."

There's no room for argument there. A day that begins with a sky-shattering sunrise and a long overdue spurt of creative energy is bound to be a good day. A novel that kicks off with a gripping first line holds onto a reader straight through to "The End." A seed that's watered and tenderly ministered just might bloom insanely.

Both blessed and bedeviled, poets are the undisputed masters of beginning and beginning again. That first sound. And every breath that reaches the page is important. That first line. That damned first stanza. The next poem. That first sound again. Gotta make that bellow necessary. Gotta hone that hook. Open that book, settle down with that opening page.

Let's have a look at some of the ways Matt Morton begins:

> The manner in which one begins is of utmost importance.

> For each moment, you are given exactly one chance,
> it is irrevocable, that is where the pressure comes from.
> —"Elegy for My Brother in the Wilderness"

> How hard I have hoped for us all to not once disappear.
> Dear father, dear stone's-throw wanderer,
> stop you now this practiced fading away.
> —"Overture"

> Here are your instructions.
> Mother Nature, apparently,
> has revised the curriculum again.
> —"Fever Dream"

> A kiss is a kind of breath: a form of breathing. And buried
> beneath the desire, an idea: of permanence, of *remainder*.
> It is how we have learned to navigate the rivers.
> —"Quebec City"

Pretty much anyone, especially harried judges, will tell you that stellar beginnings, those ravenous hooks, do not necessarily stellar poems make. But in Matt Morton's case, these compelling lines are just— well, the beginning. What follows are poems of arresting insight and stark assurance. What follows are the agile lines of someone who has mastered the sudden slap, the hushed lyric.

My intention was to dangle just enough bait to kindle your appetite for more.

You can thank me later.

And as much as I would like to trumpet Matt Morton as my own covetous discovery, he is by no means a nascent talent yanked from the Poulin's enviable contest coffers. His revelatory work has peppered the hallowed pages of dream journals. He has snagged one of those "ya done good" NEAs, and attended residencies where he was undoubtedly as much inspiration and teacher as student. He's an editor with a keen and discerning eye. He's been runnered-up, honorable-mentioned and otherwise lavishly lauded. The book he deserved, the one we were waiting for, was just out of reach.

And he has said, ". . . periods of uncertainty are often fruitful . . ."

Indeed.

So how did I know we had a winner?

I had walked away from the pile. I'd gone on to some semblance of a normal life for a while, to ease the pressure of a rough decision. I'd be tending to a sizzling skillet of garlic and Brussels sprouts, walking my behemoth dogs or screaming at the TV during a *Drag Race* episode. Suddenly, tantalizing, unbidden, a line from one of the dozens of unforgettable poems in *Improvisation Without Accompaniment* would pop into my head and live there.

And then another.

Another.

Lines that won't leave become poems you can't walk away from.

I surrendered to the hook.

—Patricia Smith

IMPROVISATION
WITHOUT
ACCOMPANIMENT

Republic

Again the chorus gathers on the stage.
      Again *again* because what does not tend
      toward repetition, in hopes of prolonging its stay?

Each day begins by promising a clear-cut expedition, but
      by evening I find myself perplexed, unsure of what
      meaning means, or why *meanness*—which means

differently—so easily enters the heart
      but takes a lifetime to root out. Finite
      infinitives: to sail, to sing, to sigh. If I seem to be

fascinated by trains, it is because I was born
      on a desert planet where there were none, oh to speed
      through evergreens in search of a focal point . . .

We assemble from our succession of voyages *history*—
      as in the reenactment, in which each god chooses a side.
      Here in our country, yesterday's wordless communiqué

consisted of merely one siren, either it warned
      of imminent airstrike or it hinted at a less radical
      change of pace, as when the flow of traffic stops

and you know it is safe to proceed, tethered
      to whichever plan has been assigned to you. *But if only*
      improvisation were permitted I could finally give my soliloquy and then

Again the moonlight filters through the sieve
      of limbs. Again the passengers fall asleep in their
      bunks on the bullet train, which plays its part

in shuttling us from one place to the next. How
        like models of courage they must have been—
        the gods who, being gods, had so little to lose.

1

Improvisation Without Accompaniment

In the field, the tractor spins its giant wheels.
How fierce defiance is, or seems. Mechanical
in a sense: our pistons firing to set aflame
some teepee of longed-for brush, this being
hope's kindling. Just once, I'd like to witness
beavers constructing a dam out of fallen
timber, dead limbs crooked and bent. I'd like
a roan horse, a wide-open pasture to ride across.
Laughter. A bottle of cheap wine. These acres
of heartland filling up with snow and snow and—
for our next trick, what will be expected of us?
The chromosomes divide with such precision.
This is the part where the origin myths diverge.
Give me something gold to grapple with: three
apples to juggle, a scrap of paper to fold
into a dove. I have seen pigeons nesting atop
the steel beams in the station, as the trains arrive
and depart, come and go. All I want to do is sit
on the porch at evening, in a pinewood rocking
chair, and watch the desert sun melt over the hills.
But it is this notion of *now* that gives me
trouble. There is no parachute, and that is sad.

The Good Life

At times, I would like a manual.
A prewar woodshop textbook. Instructions
in Esperanto for how to assemble
the clearance furniture, the horrible pink table
and chairs, that winter the only set we could afford.
By *at times* I meant *always*. At times,
I would like to save a famous soloist
from choking on her sirloin. I would like
my overnight train to evaporate in a forest
of fog and pines. Wasn't there something shiny
and small we buried there and forgot? A number
on a napkin to call when things got bad?
The dining room would erupt in cheers,
but being noble never suited anyone.
Remember our elation at the balloon animals?
Green mouse, turquoise giraffe, how they seemed
like a kind of magic, blown-up and spun
out of air, which later we learned was a kind
of emptiness. By *suited* I meant *saved*.
Outside it's raining again, and inside
I'm talking to you about the weather again
like new neighbors stuck in an elevator,
or the old couple, married for fifty years
this October, together so long they've forgotten
how not to read each other's minds.
I would like to get my hands on whatever manual
they used. There is a time for smelling the roses,
and it is not as often as you think. The fly needs help
unsticking from the web, so too the limbo'd
mosquito preserved in a chunk of amber.
I would like to pretend I don't know
what's going to happen to us when we disappear.

I know I used to drive through my neighborhood
after dark with a girl who was always fiddling
with the radio dial and talking about the weather,
the streamer clouds overhead backlit by the moon.
It may or may not be helpful to return.
Driving down the quiet street where you grew up,
the tiny homes, their orange rectangles of light.

Windfall

I see your face in a dream, distantly. A different shore:
therefore a different hour, though time is the same. Water
the same, roundabouts at least. Love: sometimes a copper
bottle discovered among the reeds. At others, at odds:
the remnants of a star, mere fragments. And if this
is happiness, then what. And if not joy, therefore. A painted
fingernail, a blue toothbrush. Dust. Here are my hands reaching
for your hands. A bunting, a lark: What will we offer? Summer
satchels and rain as if from a fountain, boardwalk smiles. Ash-
in-waiting. Miles and miles of sand with no trees: that is a desert.
This weather talk, thunder clamoring for attention, cloud cover
not if I can help it. Here: my notes for the film. Your gown,
dark as in mourning. A tower of cardboard boxes labeled
with black marker. Directions to the old house, cobblestone,
three Japanese maples seasoned red. A separation in name only:
via telephone. Sun wave-woken, land between coasts. And that
is a whole country. It will be a silent film, and the last one.

Not the Wind, Not the View

Two thousand miles away from here, my father
is lying in a strange room, being tended to.
It is always getting later. No matter
if morning is dampening the earth,
or burnt orange evening rending itself apart,
the doldrums of afternoon stuck in between.
This morning, I was sifting through
a famous nearly-dead novelist's letters,
wondering why he'd kept them all
so neatly filed away. I wasn't certain,
but I had an idea. An idea
cannot fix a heart. It cannot douse
a house on fire, which earlier I thought
my neighbor's was, but no, he was burning
wood in his backyard. Right now, I'm heating
a frozen dinner. In the studio next door
a woman is singing, and a voice on the radio
is trying to resuscitate itself beneath layers
of static. I had an idea that each day seems
the same, yet somehow shorter.
Slight variances in the weather,
rhythmic substitutions in the traffic's pulse.
I'm not sure what, but something
is long overdue. Do you understand
what it is I am saying? Somewhere
in America my father is dying and I am
sitting here, listening to the radio.

Wavelength

That feeling won't fit in a tackle box.
It won't sit still in a safe. Impossible,
you'd think, for a single dream to reopen the wound
cauterized by years, until the figure emerges
cinematically from the tree-line swept with fog.
You haven't slept in days. As it turns out
no one made you king, although the lights illuminate
the boardwalk precisely where you pass.
Each morning, inexplicably, a murder of crows
comes flocking across the dunes. You watch
from the window, horrified by the horizon.
White noise signals what's approaching. A shadow
falls across your beach read. Try not to worry.
Odds are it's someone else's turn, so you work
the jigsaw puzzle, the pieces all sea and sky.
Memorize some lines of eighteenth-century verse.
Curse your deity of choice, or blame your father
for what he failed to say, but don't forget
that the average stature of man makes
climbing most trees an impossible task.
That there is no fifth chamber inside the human heart.
Soon we'll be leaving this city for good,
though it seems we've just arrived.
I'm sorry, I too was coaxed out of hiding
under the impression that things would be greener.
I too was told there would be a chorus of bells.

Pinwheel Floating on Water

There is a feeling you may attach to the experience
of sunbathing. Of watching a landmark go up in flames.
Perhaps it is a question of tone, like the various forms
a snowflake may assume as it falls apart in your hand.
Paper lantern, silver dollar. Betrayed by his father,
the boy dumps his box of marbles down a storm drain.
Bluebonnets overwhelm an overpass. A charred field,
a swan. For years, the smell of vanilla may remind you
of a large hole in the earth. Little far-flung black star.
Is it just me or is there something about riding a train.
Ever since you were a child. You will store his ashes
inside a stoppered flute. I have nothing more to say
on the subject of disappearing. Bright light, white light.
It is the dead of winter, it is strawberry season. Here,
sit down with us. We are waiting for the show to begin.

Improvisation Containing Trace Elements

Dust-speckled, the morning
      light perforated by vinyl blinds—today
      I will refrain from mentioning black holes
although they must exist because

science says, because each of us
      freezes just on the edge of vanishing.
      In the middle of the journey of our life I found
my love in a moonlit wood then woke

alone to an absence of arrows lodged in my chest.
      A minor disappointment. Yet it lingers,
      useless as the blue rubber band which, circling
a wrist, recalls some pressing engagement

long since passed. The guidebook suggests
      a hike around the volcano's obsidian rim.
      The spoon-swirled cream assumes a Rorschach form.
All the while on the cavern wall

dance the fire-thrown shadows of what we do
      not want to know. Dear reader, don't tell me
      you've never dreamt of marching beside a stranger
across a sagebrush prairie, toward the distant

frontier. Maybe you spent without knowing it
      your morning searching for arrows, struggling
      to glean *what?* from the negative space. My advice:
if you find yourself off-route in an icy couloir,

consider the implications before
        you proceed. How a wolf will patrol the fence-line
        of its enclosure, plotting escape entirely unlike
ourselves, we who are not animal.

And the Mountains Grew Sirens

It was her lavender hands,
the wrinkles soft like crinkled cellophane, and the valley
where we stayed full of log cabins, yellow tents,
schools of rainbow trout shimmering the pond.
Like a shepherd's crook the moon
guarded us, a tear in the canvas of dark, throwing
light on the nervous mares stamping
the stable muck. The pines, all the pines glossed
with milk. Glued to her side by the window,
studying wings. Flash of sky: blue jay. Blacktop smeared
with blood: red-winged blackbird. I wondered aloud,
overwhelmed by the whoosh of the highway
cars curling out of sight down the hill.
And the clifftop triplet of crosses strung up by some hiker
with aspen and twine. Bodiless. Looming like
an empty well. She showed me
but then that night. Her face,
no one saw me see her face, its light burning out.
She was not a deer in the meadow then she was
a ghost. A skipping stone
makes circles, but a body makes a stone.
They washed the lavender off
the pillowcases. They caught me looking for her
by the piano, and if it wasn't her why else
would the middle pedal stick halfway down like that.
What is left over is less than before.
The word for that is *stop*. Forever
my dad said, which was a zooming out. I was small,
they wouldn't let me see when the curtain closed. The black
between stars, up and far away. They said *God* but
when they sang their eyes were shut. But if
prayer. I held my brother's hand and we stood

when they stood, and I could see it
leaning on them, heavy their carrying hands
when they passed in the aisle. But did she stop. Then
and there I made myself, all the streaming-in light
stained by paint on the glass. And the snow
erased the Indian paintbrushes and the birds
went with her, the field where
no one walked, all a rushing, like bats,
the storm of her going.

Overture

How hard I have hoped for us all to not once disappear.
Dear father, dear stone's-throw wanderer,
stop you now this practiced fading away.
I do not think the sun will smile again ever
if your going leaves merely
a man-shaped space, a small black hole in the air.
And you, o love, you caught uncatchable mare,
barefoot walking our makeshift northern pasture—
if now is only, and tomorrow comes lickety-
split without us having a say,
then come to me now
with your fragile butcher paper hands,
your wind-harried bent-over cattail body,
your mind ablaze firing dawn wherever you move.
We are all-in, us two. We are
deepening royal blue with darkling hymns.
But where oh where will we roost
when it starts to snow and makes impassable muck
of our what-for gravel road through the crooked mountains?

Viewfinder

Listen: there is no use looking back: and yet how
madly we want to find ourselves moored, storm-

wrecked, stranded on sandbar-moments we forgot
to notice the first time around: like a summer-
turned-fall afternoon, riding the Ferris wheel with

a face I no longer remember, and the city sprawled out
flat like a map on a tabletop: as of late, it has become

increasingly clear to me that a photograph preserves,
freezes nothing, makes nothing stay, the way saying
nothing is itself nothing special, brings nothing back:

right now, somewhere in Maryland, a woman's voice
is faltering in a confessional, now she is crying: a boy

carves circles with a stick in a fire-pit, bats crash
headlong into wind-gusts: thus, what seemed like
a pattern is rearranged: these tiny monuments—

a sand sculpture, a block of ice—were they too worth
some of our attention, like the bugles echoing out

over snow-covered fields? behind us, the years have
slackened off like a cloak from the shrugged shoulders
of someone coming in from bad weather, expecting

songs: who was it again we heard calling to us
that night in the lit-up square? this much is certain:

there will come a season when the land yields nothing,
and neither you nor I will be around to see it, to comment
on the absence of color: but there was a moment

when you were sitting beside me, so close I could have
plucked a fleck of paint from your green flannel shirt,

and this too had a place in the card catalogue of small
satisfactions, the stack of grayscale Polaroids, trinket
cars brought home from the county fair and arranged

with care on the mantelshelf: though none of it ever
took on weight, not really, not the way we hoped:

more like a mirage, a fever dream, before the framework
collapsed beneath our feet: no one to blame, no guilt
necessary, and hardly anyone if anyone around at all

to look in the eyes, as if to say, yes, yes, I have loved you,
not knowing how little it mattered, how much it meant.

2

Self-Portrait as Oswald's Ghost
Addressing the Warren Commission

Well first of all for the record I was a boy
I rode the trains underground with my face
pressed against the front car window and I could
not have been closer without falling into it
the darkness in front of all the people watching
from the platform which is to say we were racing
past faster always them wearing their anonymous
faces no doubt practiced or perhaps it was me who
was anonymous in their eyes only you see sirs
if I may it was this that I wanted to be included in
what is known to us as history I have read many
books on the subject stepping into my own role
the way you might feel the temperature of a
doorknob before turning it and entering a room
as if a man could this way make a sort of covenant
with the world so that no matter what he did or did
not do it would be marked down and permanent
like how I was a boy sitting with my mother nights
and the screen's blue flickering or for another
example take the spy planes I am a veteran do not
forget it I have been to Japan and Moscow how
the sleek chrome planes fired off the cruiser and
vanished into the secret altitudes and all of it a life
connected by a pattern drawn on the land a code
as if planted there some time before me conspiring
to lead me through a life that wasn't mine at all
but a series of events which from the start had the
name Lee Marina would say Lee do you love me
and the pattern waiting there to okay sirs yes I see
you want to know you are asking if it was me

shot him and that sirs is hard a very indeed difficult
question because say my right index finger was
poised on the trigger and the sun glinting off
the overpass and although it was November
the grass somehow green and once in Ft. Worth
it's funny I was a Texas boy see once I held
a can of coke as cold as solid ice up to my cheek
and I rode trains with my face touching darkness
and if this all happened truly to me your question
then has implications going beyond what
you are asking because what is one man really
when all of my life was this question asking
itself over again which was is there someone
helping me do these things I was and me hoping
certain history was something a man could become
though all the time afraid I was acting alone

Fever Dream

Here are your instructions.
Mother Nature, apparently,
has revised the curriculum again.
But change isn't so bad,

so bad . . . Still, there is this list
of chores to be tackled,
first of all to think
of the pesky snow collecting

in little white mounds
on the gutters and shingles.
And did you see the news? The paper
claims the morgue is to be

shut down for good. It's all I can do
to try to keep
the variables straight, to blow up
the balloons, light the candles.

Sometimes it's a bit like spelunking.
Sometimes it resembles pinball-bumpers
left on autopilot. *It's all the same*
is an incorrect mantra

you will be tempted to adopt.
Help me, o stranger, I have abandoned
my true love in the garden.
Even now, lounging in my slippers, I feel

something grand is expected of me.

Improvisation After Keats

This living hand could do anything.
It could spray-paint my brother's name
on an overturned canoe, skip teal stones
across the Brazos, or pour skim milk
on a bowl of shredded wheat,

which might be more consequential
than it sounds. Delight can be drawn
from the smallest things. A flurry
late in the season. The taste, the first
in years, of ginger ale. But these pale

when measured against the gleaming
monolith the mind constructs in sleep,
or daydreams in the striped awning's shade.
This heart, so warm and capable, will break
but once, so why this urge to bellow

into a carnival megaphone, startling
a kit of pigeons into the night sky?
If only we could sail to a secret archipelago,
or simply press a button to shore up
a crystalline future, the one we have

longed for, and almost deserve . . .
See how the half-moon hangs like a broken
pact above the deserted Midway aisles?
If you stop, if you squint at the carousel,
the metal horses could almost be alive.

All Honeycombed, the Ground

Lately, a whole host of problems: the morning paper
filled with missed connections, fender benders clotting
the iced-over highway. Reports of ghosts go unconfirmed
and my best student emails me to say she's afraid to talk
in class and doesn't know why. As for me, I have for
a stretch been a stranger to myself, riding the carousel
with you I did not know who I was. Meanwhile, winter

paws around the city, turning up the roots of stubborn
flowers. The body falls apart like leaves. A woman knows
how to sail, then one day cannot remember how to sail.
Perpetual travel solves nothing: Here vs. There when
all the while the earth is a giant stone sent skipping
over nothingness. Most of us will never observe
a polar bear in its natural habitat. Love is perplexing

at best. Most of us will have to be reminded. *The rest
of you can all go to hell*. The ax-murderer was a happy child
and you were a child and I was the child with a secret
in the cross-legged circle, sitting in front of the gilded altar.
Our parents smiled and watched as we were told stories.
In the church, after hours: clangs of hand-bell practice.
In the penny kaleidoscope I saw spotted horses.

Quebec City

A kiss is a kind of breath: a form of breathing. And buried
beneath the desire, an idea: of permanence, of *remainder*.
It is how we have learned to navigate the rivers. The view
of the sea from the hilltop was limited in scope and
there is no other like it, will not be. Can't go back there:
a haze like a curtain of fog, which obscured the boats,
the little boats that had gathered in the bay. But there are plenty
of cities to visit, cornucopias arranged on tables.
Why were we afraid to ask the tourist to take our photograph
on the wharf? Not a tidal wave, not even a bee sting.
An idea: of bronze statuary, of *epitaph*. It is how we have learned
to fall asleep. City as spin room, as whirlpool. Remember
the morning I bought you a red balloon at the foot of the castle.
A kiss, a curtain of mist: a certainty. "It does not satisfy me, or,
I am not satisfied." *Because it can't be true. Because it can't be true.*

Pale Annual

Now it is winter, this is the waiting part.
Like low-dangling tinsel, eraser-gray—the sky
has been stripped of its shingles. A swath

of off-white, a lack of shimmering. Look
at the sun removed from its element, a violet-
tinged sheet of old foil, bereft, balled-up

and stuck on a fishhook. This time of year
again, its hallway drafts. Season
of spendthrifts, twinkling lights, wishful thinking.

It is true that things have at times been hell,
your head like a dynamite tunnel
blown through granite. But so what if joy

is not a precious stone, not perfectly
smooth as we were led to believe it would be?
Nevertheless, the cold days dwindle

beneath the cracked white plate
of a face—the blank sky, which is
nearly obscured by our idea of a sky. It emits

a dull ringing, like a teaspoon tapping
methodically against the glass dome of a snow globe.

Wintering

Bulletbored, I stayed in bed.
So wrongly ever seemed to churn things out!
Grand old waterspout coming my way
I sing and sang to my half-broke brain.
Rather be spruce-bowered under a sun
than dead, but the cold world's rather made as if
a hundred ghosts are asking up
and down the aisles of a blacked-out train,
whether I never liked them around or not.
Back there, far behind me? I splashed.
Time was, I held a woman laughing,
happy and sunmottled all in the waves and
cresting castles moated blue around us.
Wide open, time was. Bodies ago,
till now. Now, he's a lonely pup
who thrashes filthy, like so: night through night,
I up and dream my downstairs thoughts,
while across the wallpaper lightning creeps
its fiery tarantella. Truth:
if this is not hell it quite resembles it.
If I didn't feel so hapless small I'd flee all
vows, all crystal hymns, all—Oh, I see.

Telltale

They spin at the top of the Ferris wheel, the children
were spinning. I am poking my eye
through a penpoint hole in the bottom of a Styrofoam cup.
Like an orange, it peels away
from my teeth, my mouth filling up
with little white canoes. Midnight, and we found new
antlers hanging on the wall, shadows hanging on the wall
behind them cast by the yellow moon hanging outside
the glass. The ceiling ribboned and bowed.
Cast at the peak, cast at the peak.
What sails sings
through the air, flies over the flung-
across surface in the general direction of swans. Blue
not black like the barrel with pumpkinseed floating,
where my head shoved, my mouth filling up
with scales and fins, with nothing,
the nothing sour and wet on my tongue. I must say,
the frogs in the yard, I must say.
But the sun, warm on the white skin on my arm,
and my bare feet touching cool dirt,
walking on the soft green needles. *Ting*
the hidden bird *Ting* like tapping the silver triangle
like dangling upside down among springtime leaves,
shins shining in light.
I was the king of deserts, I cradled a little glacier
under my tongue. The fraction of an inch
where the sand dune meets the sea, that,
that is the salt I was talking about
exactly! Me and my brother found
a bronze key on the ground under the aspen.
No, not with my eyes closed.
In the meadow, the aspens

dropping gold in the quiet in the snow.
But you are my brother but there is a ghost on your face
I said. You said listen the chimes have
and then we were running with the scarecrow
on our heels the face the yarn hair sliced off coming
from its mouth stuck open gaping, and my mouth filling up
with the soundlessness we were running
across the meadow away from
the legs the terrible wound and she
was running and we were running and the sawdust
is running out behind her across the field.

Vardaman

My brother is Darl. He went to Jackson on the train.

I saw my brother crying on the box
where my mother is. A big moon
sawed in half above him crying for
what my mother took with her when
she left the day. Where did she go
I asked my brother. It is always
night where she is he said.
My brother's head is full of flames.
I can't see them. I can see two blue
circles like holes of sky punched through
a fence and why is there no smoke.
One day I found something she wrote.
I showed my brother and he took it
and he said you can keep a secret good
so I knew it was something
that could be mine and his but not for my father
and not for my mother. My brother's brain
is wrong but my brother is right. It was night
when he went on the train. The sun is on fire
too and it runs on tracks too. First
it is night and then it goes up up and over
and then it goes down and then
it is night again. Time
must run on tracks too because it goes
in a big circle and that is why clocks.
A clock is a long time
and it is also a short time. I have
to do all the not-telling myself now.
Crying on the box of my mother
under a moonhalf. Bright blue holes

of shining. One day I'll go in a box
too with night in it like my mother
and my mother will be there
and we will get on a red train
and ride through the night trees and black
leaves with moon on them
to where my brother is
waiting in the cool air
with no more fire inside his head.

Improvisation in an Alpine Field

After months of snow-mantled mountains, spring.
This evening the meadow—the hard ground
which, last week, you would have sworn would never
again give way to flowers—is blotched pink
with hundreds of Indian paintbrushes, which resemble
neither blood, nor confetti, nor fire, though you often
hear them described this way.

                               This way. What do we mean
when we say that? A heretofore hidden road, perhaps,
a game-trail of mud and hoof-pressed grass through
a stretch of nettles and briars to an open field
where the flowers have bloomed again, simply,
like flowers, to be picked apart by the mule deer feeding
at dusk. *If you could be any animal*

                                 the question begins,
and as with most questions, the answer—
perhaps a stallion, an owl—matters significantly
less than the person you have asked, he or she being
the climate, you might say, which the question inhabits,
just as you might say the field gives context
to the paintbrushes, which ask, or seem to ask,
something now of us, we who have hiked here to marvel
at the bare, reared heads.

                          As if the earth existed
for this sole function of sacrifice, to offer us
whatever shape or color we desired. As if desire,
like the blazing flowers and the mindless silhouettes
of deer, were itself perennial, and we—after years
of starting out, of setting forth, and finally having arrived
at this particular unspectacular stretch of land—

might now be granted some measure of clemency
and could lie still, never again to anticipate watching
the people we love disappear.

3

Elegy for My Brother in the Wilderness

1.

The manner in which one begins is of utmost importance.

For each moment, you are given exactly one chance,
it is irrevocable, that is where the pressure comes from.

It is necessary, first, to reconcile yourself with the stars, which pose
as beacons but are all gas and fire,
nothing with which you could acquaint yourself
if given the chance, see, you would burn right up.

And still the echo of dripping water inside the cavern.
And still the blazing sun, prepared for the party.

Perhaps to begin in a mountain meadow, with two boys
watching a stag graze thistle,
its adolescent horn-stubs starting to show.

2.

All loosey-goosey in the suburbs, we lit Chinese lanterns
and watched them expand and trend upward, toward orbit.

Yours was made of red paper. It inhaled
the fire like smoke from a joint and we held our breaths

as it rose, then caught in an oak-crook, a leaf canopy,
dislodged itself and flew over the chimneys

and shingled roofs. When someone from a passing car
chucked a pumpkin at us—it was Halloween—

we picked up the broken halves
and, laughing, pressed them to our faces, like masks.

It was like reality masquerading as dream.
It was like a festival of our own creation.

3.

As in the story when Actaeon, hunting in a snowy wood,
glimpsed between white aspen trunks
the bare shoulders of the goddess, just out of reach.

Even in the myth the dogs had names—Laelaps,
Theron, Hylaeus—he had raised them up as pups,

hunting with them so often he no longer recognized them
as his own: they had become like paintings
hung in an entryway for guests to admire, not for

the one who has hung them and quickly forgets,
moving on to other things.

Thus, when the hounds began to bellow, as if in warning,
it startled him—he had forgotten
where he was and racing forward he thought to himself

no, no something is not right

and shocked with dread electric
he came upon that which he had sought
without even knowing it, the woman—cloaked

in nakedness, water running down
her pale arms—who turned from him

just as he felt himself begin to change.

4.

In my dream of the garden party, everyone was there:

four armored knights-errant were there searching
for the Queen who was not present she had
marked the date wrong on her calendar
or her handlers had forgotten

Charlie Chaplin was there he refused to mingle
no one was surprised to see Walt Whitman there in a dashing suit
the Messiah was rumored to be there

Henri Matisse had set up an easel off in a corner as had
Vincent van Gogh who arrived with Theo

Stalin was turned away at the door he had not been invited
it was a matter of great scandal and rightly so and

soon everyone was dancing the flamenco a minuet a square dance
while onstage I juggled wearing a blue button-down shirt

when you arrived and the dream suddenly
changed you were the center of attention

telling jokes pretending your mind was not orbiting elsewhere
your hands in your pockets your presence

like a question I had
not heard and was nevertheless expected to answer

5.

In one of the many cities where you are not,

The little alcoves, like something from the Old World, punctuating
    the cobblestone streets,
The dimly lit balconies, their cast-iron railings adorned with red
    ribbon,
The girls walking arm-in-arm with other girls, wearing vine-patterned
    dresses and black dresses,
The full moon dressed for the occasion, which has been agreed upon
    by everyone, though no one knows precisely what is to be
    commemorated, who is in charge, or where the party is,
The streets alive with rumors, with men in love and women in love,
    with drunken laughter,
The old woman wearing a spotless apron selling pastries out of a cart
    on a corner, the bored horse shaking its mane,
The candle-lit café tables, the waiters and waitresses with their
    practiced approaches and kitchen gossip, their cigarette kisses
    in back alleyways,
And through the narrow spaces between the bakeries and the shops
    and the apartment buildings,
The sea, which, once seen, one can never forget.

6.

Why have you renounced me I said

You uprooted my tree he said

I only meant to build a bridge I said

You laughed at my frontier diorama he said

I wanted to protect you from witches I said

You closed the gate on my arm he said

I did not know myself I said

You said if you wanted to kill me you could he said

I was only a boy I said

And I was only a boy he said

In my dreams you are always outside the window I said

You coughed during my recital he said

There was a bee in my throat I said

You put it there on purpose he said

I am sorry it was in the script I said

I am sorry it was in the script he said

7.

Like a cracked statuette,

Like the blue crepuscule, like the song I faintly
      hear from the other side of the river that divides us,
           ice floes knocking against one another, against the shore,

Like the demarcated seasons which nevertheless come and go of their
      own accord,

Like a Chopin nocturne, a construction-paper ship halved by child-
      size scissors, a smaller-than-expected harvest of wheat,

Like the running thread in a collar, like a sputtering trawler,
      collapsing crest of a wave,

Like a caboose on fire racing down wooden tracks,

Like the black sheep on the hillside, like the hillside, the mountain
      which has chosen, finally, to lie down,

Like the signature on the note that one discovers on a Tuesday
      after stopping at the corner grocery for a rotisserie chicken,

Like the scripted discovery of the virgin bathing in spring-water,

Like the instant when one ceases to recognize oneself,

Like the moment when one recognizes the emptiness
      of the sky, the emptiness of *sky*.

8.

As is the case with all stories, there is an alternate version,
the one the partygoers have tried to forget

in which Actaeon never stumbles upon what he sought,
but instead confronts an absence in the river—

the dumb flow of water around a boulder,
a void where something crucial should have been.

And now I do not know if it was me

who found you struggling in the water,
who called out to you although you could not hear me,

or if it was you
who discovered what you could not bear to see, an emptiness

which I—who, for years, had followed you through
the forest—could not understand.

Because, of course, there were no Chinese lanterns.

9.

Once while driving to school, I had just turned sixteen, he and I began
to argue the way that brothers argue, maybe about the radio

and when I struck his chin—hard—with the back of my fist

while navigating a curve in the road between the retirement home
and the open field, I don't know which of us was more surprised,

and I cannot forget the look on his face, which filled up
not with tears, nor fear, nor anger, but a terrible light,

as if he were standing in front of a house on fire,

because now we understood how easy it was
for me to turn on him

as one might throw out a newspaper
after skimming the headlines and seeing nothing worth the time.

And the sun shone down on the sandlot as we passed.
And my apology was like an ancient currency

in the black car in the school parking lot in
the town where it never
snowed it being a Texas town where we often joked

that nothing of importance ever happened.

4

Spring Bulletin

Then, one afternoon, the sirens stopped.
Soon after, spring resurrected itself as bluebonnets,
new styles. Jazz was back that year,
the blues was out. Everywhere: sunlight on bare knees.
Still, winter spoke to us sometimes
through its lexicon of vanishings, its lingering pull
of icicles like phantom limbs on trees. Something
vaguely unsettling about the quality of air.
Something about the humidity that left us
glancing over our shoulders when we mowed the lawn.
Now that we could go outside again,
one wondered as a result: Should I buy that ticket
to the mountains? Should I become a postman after all?
Or should we wait a little longer,
until the telegram arrives? Yes,
we thought to ourselves, we'll sit right here. No reason
to feel guilty. It's a lot to think about—holes to paper over,
stains to scrub from dresses
never worn. On days like this one,
sitting among the trees with their makeup on, it may be normal
or not to think, *Now I see, all this time*
I have never loved anyone. Not the way they do in films,
saturated with color, wearing fancy clothes
at the beach, clutching daggers.
It's colder here than you imagined. We're always getting it wrong.
Three birthdays since you spoke
to her, and then one April morning she called: "Quick,
it's happening just like they said." How did she get this number?
Sure enough, on every channel,
the elk were walking across the bridge,
news helicopters buzzing around like flies.
In preparation, all the city's hearses lined up around the block,

each driver waiting his turn
to lay on the horn. But all you could think about
were the fireworks at the county fair,
where, years ago, you held the giant red mallet,
standing on stacked bales of hay at evening, turning first
to make sure she was watching.

The View from Here

What to make of the ridged aluminum awning
     behind the warehouse? A silver accordion?
     A model of the Swiss Alps? Where I live,
the cargo trains wrest sleepers from scenes

of Technicolor oceans, their cheeks bruised,
     their heads full of songs
     that make no sound, like the esoteric
graffiti that covers the metro station walls.

Outside, phantoms flit above the motel pool
     drained for the season and collecting leaves.
     Remember, every story has a moral.
Two lovers are wrenched apart by war

then reunited at breakfast in a chalet,
     or the weeping villagers cover a woman's head
     with a burlap sack, place the body
aboard a rowboat, and set it aflame.

In most arguments, both parties are at fault,
     so perhaps we shouldn't blame one another
     for the anxious zeitgeist—
nor God, who one day woke to find

himself transmuted into a moth. Forever
     the flames drift down the narrow channel
     toward the bay. Let us not forget to play,
to skillfully escape the handcuffs

of solemnity, the goopy entrée everyone
      feels obligated to eat. I'm sick of searching
      for my reflection in the concrete fields
behind my tenement. Better to be

combusting, unbuckled and soaring,
      watching the sun collapse beneath
      the razor-thin horizon, the violet clouds stretching out
from the window seat, like a sea of ice.

Improvisation with Scenes from the Pageant

The day had appointed itself master of ceremonies.
In the schoolyard, children prepared for the holiday
masque, everyone costumed in colonial clothes. Wildfires,
for what seemed like weeks, ate up the hillside behind

Mac's soda shop. It was like being in on a secret, like a note
stowed away in a damp oak-hollow for you to discover,
either this year or the next. Trombone troupe, photocopy,
cadaver. When you finally succeed in no longer expecting

the best, there becomes a new best. A single pink flare lit
the clouds. She said, *But these are only store-bought muffins.*
A garden snake lies axe-halved on the sidewalk. One goal
might be to whittle experience down to its basic elements.

Another, to blow up a bridge. In the case of Sylvia Plath
she wrote "Balloons," then moved on to other things.
Most accidents make sense in retrospect. I have been
to the circus on only one occasion. Rain gauge, furnace

full of diamonds. It was half-price raspberry-lemonade
night at the ballpark. When the whole complex lost power
they burned candles, and after the wedding there was a raucous
barn dance, which lasted almost as long as we had hoped.

City at Night

The avenues filled with elephants on parade.
Three kinkajous in uniform stood guard
atop a red construction crane. The giraffes—
recently returned from eating lobster,
still wearing stained bibs—lined the curbs.
Someone said, *The only thing missing is fireworks*

and, what do you know, the sky began
to explode and brightly wilt with sparks and ash.
Even the distant stars, dim though they were,
made a cameo appearance, hanging like ornaments
over the children, who clutched their mothers' hands.
Couples kissed beneath lights strung-up between
frosted skyscrapers. Secretly, everyone wondered
where it all had come from, and what strange
episode would happen next. That's when

the dogs and cats turned up out of nowhere
in regal attire, and performed a skit poking fun
at the Revolution. There was dancing, it was
choreographed to perfection. Imagine that!
It was truly spectacular. Then it was over.
And I was there, and you were there, and you.

Landscape

How like a forest fire is the heart.
I find it difficult, exceedingly. And who
somehow in sixty whirling years will be—
to coldly comfort one another—left?
I am bereft and are you heaven-sent
hope all the shes and hes in Valparaiso
and Marrakesh and snowy Turin.
Once I was pleased in a meadow to meet
myself, and carefully I ever after
have been like a hunter tracking him
through vales of greensward shadow
and timberline passes of rock,
pausing nightly to greet with great politeness
yonder moon. I have, in the highlands, mined
that it is good to begin slate-blank each day
anew—to leaping wake with a start and count
one's crooked blessings.
The very least of which not being
how I, in history's neighborhood, am here
for now, glowing. Thus it commences,
lightly, to rain. Like him before me
I tip my hat to you.

The Idea

Attend to what melts: what redly blooms, then wilts.
A sort of heart-monitor, a sizing up. Do not try
however to iron the wrinkles out of the ocean,
as if happiness could fit in a peacoat pocket. The idea
is to be always leaving the outdated versions behind.
For instance: I was a weed impersonating a dragon,

then I was bruised but alive in the go-cart wreckage.
When I say *ocean* I mean big water-filled canyon. The idea
is to notice: cairn of stones on the tundra, whistling
kettle, antler-scarred bark. I know moderation is
the wisest course, but how difficult when I see your face
not to smash my guitar on the coffee table and sing.

Improvisation Ending in Jamais Vu

What I miss I find
eventually frosted in silence,
in my pocket pulled out of yesterday's wash
with the Budapest key ring, the rusted quarters,
the penny with no face. There are moments
that melt like snow through finger ravines, and moments
that stand stock-still in the street. Live wires
fallen across the bridge, dead wasp twitching on the path.
Trench coat full of chocolate bars and nails. Thank you,
she kept saying to me, thank you
for sliding the noose from my neck.
All winter we lay in the swing.
All that practice writing gibberish with a glow stick in the sand,
still I spill the song like wine across the sheet.
All the photographs candle-curled.
But tell me again my favorite part
where the waited-for, barely believed-in shining thing
emerges from the forest fire,
the secret draped around its neck. Divine
as waking to a hand against your cheek and autumn
drifting through the punctured screen . . . From the refrigerator,
blue construction paper waves. Dust settles over
the plastic sofa coffins in our home.
No time is worth the price of nothingness.
O my city, your colors and sounds and
all the blinking lights, hello,
we've come back! For years, I walked blindfolded
by their white and black checkerboard scarf, but on the day
the piñata burst and hummingbirds brilliantly
swarmed from the entry wound,
believe me, at that instant my stature was
of such little worth—in the wet green grass I sat

and wept at the sky rising over the hills,
the farmhouses and furrowed fields,
as paint ran down the trunks of the elms
I had seen, camouflaged, so many times before.

The Expedition

It's not a tragedy. We knew this
but were always forgetting. It was comforting
to imagine an audience for our predicament,
which somehow made the problem seem
smaller, a peripheral smudge in a grand panorama
observed by a solemn sentry
perched on a cloud. It is tempting—
sitting on a red plush seat in a rattling train compartment,
watching the windowed countryside rush in
and out of view—to conceive of yourself
as an actress. A wind-up soldier. A prisoner
on the verge of peripeteia. But this, too,
was confusing: how we swore to ourselves
we wanted to be selfless. Wasn't it always our own interests
that interested us? The weeks we spent
writing noble epitaphs. The way the harpist's arpeggio
in the marbled concert hall drowned out
the bombs driven into lobbies overseas.
Perhaps we shouldn't be so hard on ourselves.
After all, each nascent day nudges the sun
toward another superficial conclusion.
We got older when we weren't looking.
We woke up in a foreign city, wringing our hands.
It is true that *acceptance* sometimes feels like
standing on a shoestring strung across a gorge,
but isn't the balancing act itself the game plan
we've been looking for, a strategy for ignoring the subtext
of afternoon? Sometimes, it helps
to have a reminder. Maybe you were drinking
espresso with a friend in a retro café,
discussing the implications of an ancient dialogue
when suddenly the solution crystallized, the brilliance

of the irony struck you again: this big project
of self-making we embarked on years ago,
without quite understanding what it was.
Countless dress rehearsals, hours
spent buttressing our mirrored egos,
frantically rechecking the inventoried rations, only to learn
the very thing called for was not a skyward climb,
but a stripping away.
Because, for our purposes, the view *is* there
to be taken in—neon arboretums, ghost town
theater marquees, dust devils, prairie squalls
and all the mountains hurtling up into pink
and blue clouds. It's okay to enjoy
the shifting kaleidoscope of scenery,
to sit still and be quiet
for a while, settling into our roles once more
on this, our journey west, toward the sea.

Improvisation on Federal Hill

Baltimore

Today the sky, dappled with white clouds,
  resembles a novelty cake at a neighborhood bake sale.
  "Sky-blue cake" may verge on precious, the way

"I do not want to be sad" is sentimental because
  something crucial has been left out. The challenge is
  to grasp what's *there* before it boards a bus or drowns,

before the truth about one's parentage is revealed.
  Have you seen that play? Like an off-color joke
  it gets under your skin, the courthouse, lit-up for the festival,

suddenly small. The challenge is to open oneself
  to uncertainty, to negative capability, as in *At the end*
  of the dimly lit hall is a circular table, on which

sits a lamp with red lampshade and an unplugged rotary phone
  that has started to ring. At the end Keats wrote,
  "I have left no immortal work behind me,"

and then he was no longer Keats.
  When the clouds runneth over they are no longer clouds,
  they are like music insofar as they swell and swell

before bursting. The challenge is to narrow yourself
  toward an unfiltered version, a vinyl recording
  of your dream diary, your stump speech improvised

with all the field sounds left in—a wind-whipped flag,
　　　an all-night diner waitress repeating your order:
　　　"You do not want to be sad, you want to revise yourself

in the direction of gliding sans friction,
　　　like a skate." Like the cloud-cake. Like the freighter,
　　　which slices across the otherwise motionless harbor.

Dialectic

Back then, I always felt I was on the edge
of something. A boulder half-submerged
in the Adriatic, a ridge overlooking the plains.
I was a pioneer and didn't want to be.
In one dream I ran from tornadoes,
in another I floated through space, out past Jupiter,
body long gone, looking around at
the darkness, but with what eyes? You can't
imagine that darkness. Now I wonder
if fear is the appropriate response,
given that we are, after all, going nowhere.
Or not going anywhere. Words muddle.
Maybe we're already ghosts and don't know it
my friend said while we were losing our minds
in the park. A month later, huddled inside his Carhartt,
he watched them lower her body into the earth,
the coffin touched by snow. No, we must
be here because my phone keeps ringing,
the alarm on the egg-shaped clock on my desk
is always threatening to sing, and I can't stop
saying I'm sorry, I'm running late for the dentist,
another conference with my student
who never shows up. Maybe he knows
more than I do, sees the edge clearly
and doesn't care, as he waters tomatoes
on the roof of his building, smokes a spliff midday,
lobs a water balloon at a man's third attempt to parallel park—
Forgive me, I'm just a collection of thoughts
that buzz like newborn wasps, the sum of affects
always at war, never sure which one's on top.
Even now, I am elsewhere and running behind
but you are waiting for me where the cobblestone path

winds down to the harbor's edge. I head toward
everything lit-up and distant. Aiming for you
and the sea, I cut through drifts of fog
that hang like tinsel on the Tennessee pines.

Loomings No Longer

I was all freshly aglimmer,
wave-persuaded into a gold possibility.
At first a marsh, a murkily-seeming surface.
But magnified our practiced roles
of shrinking turned up false. And strangely so—
how the beacon of dreams we imagined
could be so easily swept aside. Now
it was *his* shadow of terror who shrank.
No, it was not the hoped-for endless
autumn stowed away, but a nevertheless
little gift, a balance beam. One half
level way to look, one half calmly steeling-oneself
in the wind. Leaves, burnt
on occasion, sharpened their edges.
The costumed sky became, merely, the sky.
I thought to my waking morning self,
Would that I might for year beyond year
discover myself just so! Because it is
after all a large fine planet, a giant sea.
I do not owe, but give thanks for
such bright and brief sufficiency.

Acknowledgments

Thank you to the editors of the journals in which these poems first appeared:

The Adroit Journal: "And the Mountains Grew Sirens";
AGNI: "Elegy for My Brother in the Wilderness";
American Literary Review: "Wavelength";
Colorado Review: "Telltale";
Columbia Journal: "Improvisation with Scenes from the Pageant," "Viewfinder";
Copper Nickel: "Improvisation on Federal Hill";
Crazyhorse: "Loomings No Longer";
Cream City Review: "Vardaman";
Devil's Lake: "Spring Bulletin";
diode: "Overture," "Fever Dream";
Drunken Boat: "Wintering";
Forklift, Ohio: "Self-Portrait as Oswald's Ghost Addressing the Warren Commission";
Gettysburg Review: "The View from Here";
Gulf Coast: "Not the Wind, Not the View";
Harvard Review: "The Expedition";
Indiana Review: "Pinwheel Floating on Water";
KERA *Art&Seek*: "Republic";
The Massachusetts Review: "City at Night";
Mid-American Review: "Pale Annual";
Nashville Review: "The Good Life";
New Orleans Review Online: "Dialectic";
Ninth Letter: "All Honeycombed, the Ground," "The Idea";
Quarterly West: "Improvisation Containing Trace Elements," "Improvisation in an Alpine Field";
Sycamore Review: "Windfall";
Tin House Online: "Improvisation Without Accompaniment";
Weave: "Improvisation Ending in Jamais Vu";

"Windfall" received the *Sycamore Review* Wabash Prize for Poetry, selected by Bob Hicok.

"The Idea" was reprinted on *Verse Daily*.

Thank you to Patricia Smith for selecting this book, and to Peter Conners and the BOA staff.

I am grateful for the financial and intellectual support provided by the National Endowment for the Arts, Johns Hopkins University, the University of North Texas, the University of Texas at Austin, the Bread Loaf Writers' Conference, and the Sewanee Writers' Conference.

Thank you to my teachers: Michael Adams, James Arthur, Bruce Bond, Jehanne Dubrow, Corey Marks, Jean McGarry, Mary Jo Salter, Alan Shapiro, Alicia Stallings, Mark Strand, David Yezzi, and Dean Young.

For their encouragement and feedback on early versions of this book, I would like to thank Callie Siskel, J. P. Grasser, Cody Ernst, Taylor Koekkoek, Joselyn Takacs, Richie Hofmann, Peter Mishler, Rosalie Moffett, Jim Redmond, and Caleb Braun.

Thank you, Lewis Fallis and Lesya Bazylewicz.

About the Author

Matt Morton is the recipient of awards from the National Endowment for the Arts, the Bread Loaf Writers' Conference, and the Sewanee Writers' Conference. His poems appear widely in such places as *AGNI*, *Gettysburg Review*, *Harvard Review*, and the *Los Angeles Review of Books*. He received his MFA from Johns Hopkins University and is currently a Robert B. Toulouse Doctoral Fellow in English at the University of North Texas.

BOA Editions, Ltd.
The A. Poulin, Jr. New Poets of America Series

Colophon

BOA Editions, Ltd., a not-for-profit publisher of poetry and other literary works, fosters readership and appreciation of contemporary literature. By identifying, cultivating, and publishing both new and established poets and selecting authors of unique literary talent, BOA brings high-quality literature to the public. Support for this effort comes from the sale of its publications, grant funding, and private donations.

❧

The publication of this book is made possible, in part, by the support of the following patrons:

Anonymous
Susan DeWitt Davie
Joe Finetti, *in memory of John F. Finetti*
James Long Hale
Keetje & Sarah Kuipers, *in honor of the birth of Lyle Wood Kuipers*
Jack & Gail Langerak
Melanie & Ron Martin-Dent
Edith Matthai, *in memory of Peter Hursh*
Joe McElveney
Boo Poulin
Steven O. Russell & Phyllis Rifkin-Russell
Sue S. Stewart, *in memory of Steven L. Raymond*
William Waddell & Linda Rubel